CAN YOU SEA ME?

A children's guide to
camouflage in the ocean

DEDICATED TO MY FAMILY FOR CULTIVATING MY LOVE OF THE OCEAN

Fedd Books
P.O. Box 341973
Austin, TX 78734

www.thefeddagency.com
Published in association with The Fedd Agency, Inc., a literary agency.

ISBN: 978-1-957616-26-1
eISBN: 978-1-957616-27-8
LCCN: 2022918592

Printed in the United States of America

CAN YOU SEE ME?

I'M A PYGMY SEAHORSE

The Pygmy Seahorse is colorful yet shy. It grows to match the color of the corals it lives on. The corals can be pink, purple, yellow, or orange. As the smallest seahorse in the world, it is only 2 centimeters long. That's the size of a peanut!

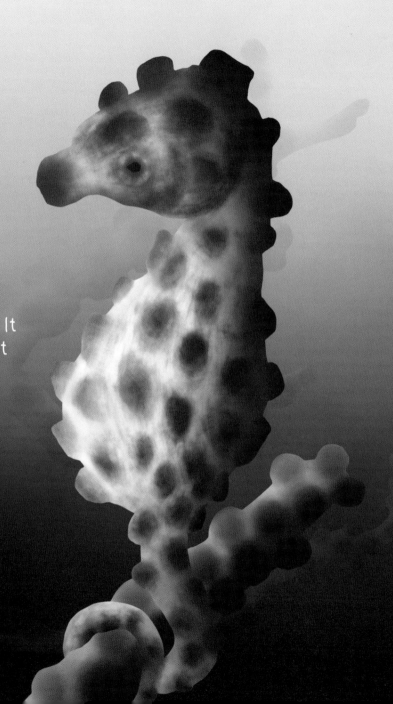

CAN YOU SEE ME?

I'M A RETICULATE WHIPRAY

The Reticulate Whipray relies on its spotted pattern and sandy environment for camouflage. Its long, whip-like tail is three times the length of its body. It also has a stinger! This whipray can weigh up to 260 pounds. That's as heavy as a baby elephant!

I'M A MOON JELLY

Although it has no brain or heart, the Moon Jelly uses thread-like tentacles covered in stinging cells to catch tiny prey. Made up of 95% water, it is see-through and often goes unnoticed. Because it is a weak swimmer, it needs ocean currents to guide it. Moon Jellies sometimes travel in large groups called "smacks," and each jelly can grow up to 7 inches in width (the length of a pencil).

I'M AN
URCHIN
CRAB

The Urchin Crab is small yet crafty. It carries sea urchins on its back for camouflage to prevent large fish from eating it. This also helps the sea urchin move around. Some sea urchins can even be venomous. When animals are venomous, they cause painful stings.

I'M A
LEAFY
SEA DRAGON

The Leafy Sea Dragon is a skilled hunter that feeds on tiny shrimp. Although it has no teeth, its long, tube-like snout slurps up its prey like a straw. Leafy camouflage and the armor-like plates covering its body prevent it from becoming a snack itself. It grows to about 8 inches in length. That's as long as a banana!

CAN YOU SEE ME?

I'M A
PEACOCK
FLOUNDER

The Peacock Flounder is a stealthy hunter that preys on crabs, shrimp, and small fish. It uses its flower-like markings and camouflage for both hunting and hiding from predators. It can even change color to match its environment. Swimming sideways on the ocean floor, the Peacock Flounder is as flat as a pancake!

CAN YOU SEE ME?

I'M A HAWKSBILL SEA TURTLE

Named for its pointed, hawk-like beak, the Hawksbill Sea Turtle feeds on toxic sponges that few animals can digest. Despite living in the ocean, it must surface to breathe air. Its dazzling shell and scales blend in with its surroundings, and its color can differ depending on water temperature.

WE ARE
GHOST
PIPEFISH

Resembling floating pieces of seaweed, Ghost Pipefish drift motionlessly over the sea floor in search of tiny shrimp. Their color can range from bright green to grey, yellow, or even pink. They are often spotted in pairs with the larger female and smaller male swimming side by side.

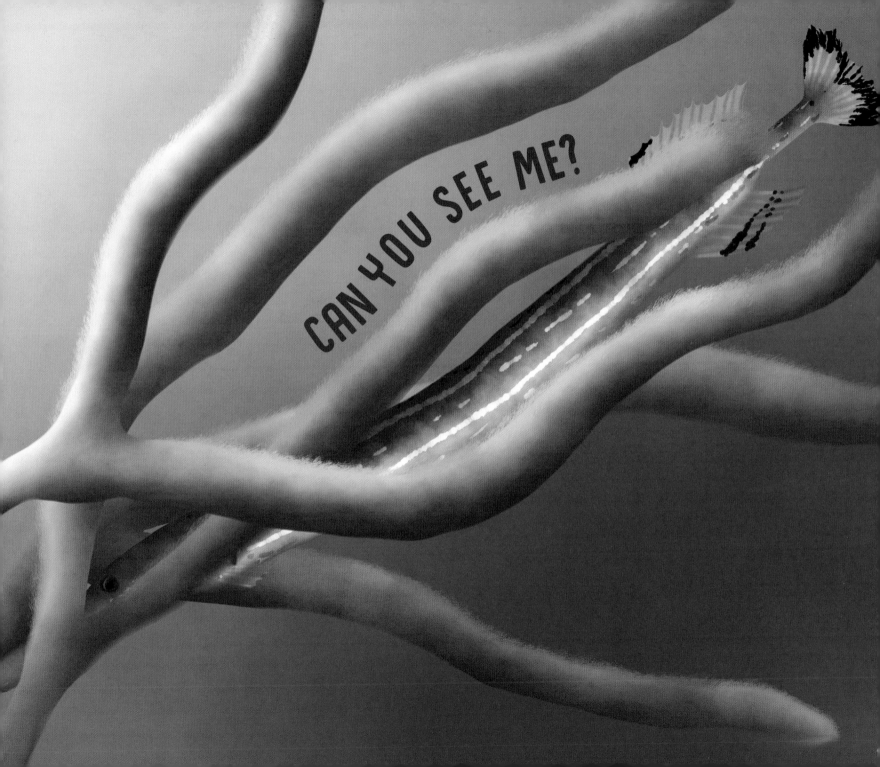

I'M A
TRUMPETFISH

The Trumpetfish is long and vibrant with a flexible jaw that stretches as wide as its body. It swims vertically among corals and sponges and can open its mouth so quickly that prey is sucked inside. When its jaw is fully extended, its mouth and face take on the appearance of a trumpet.

I'M A MIMIC OCTOPUS

Because it can change both its color and texture, the Mimic Octopus is able to impersonate a variety of animals such as sea snakes and lionfish. The creatures it mimics are often venomous, so predators avoid the octopus to keep themselves safe. Strangely enough, the Mimic Octopus has three hearts and nine brains!

CAN YOU SEE US?

I'M A SARGASSUM SHRIMP

I'M A SARGASSUM FISH

I'M A SARGASSUM CRAB

These creatures live on floating pieces of Sargassum Seaweed that provide them with shelter and protection. These species of crab, shrimp, and fish are rarely found anywhere else and are specifically camouflaged to live in this environment. They are so tiny that they could all fit in the palm of your hand!

CAN YOU SEE ME?

I'M AN
ANGEL SHARK

The Angel Shark is a patient hunter capable of waiting in one place for weeks for prey to come close enough for an ambush. Its camouflaged, sandpaper-like skin allows it to practically disappear against the sea floor, and it can grab prey as quickly as you can snap your fingers!

WHAT IS CAMOUFLAGE?

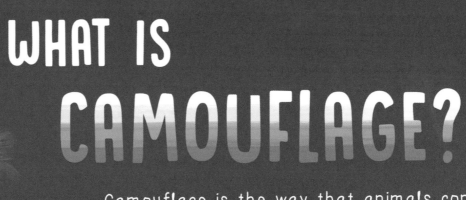

Camouflage is the way that animals conceal themselves in their environment. They hide from predators to keep themselves safe or hide from prey in order to launch a surprise attack. The four types of camouflage are concealing coloration, disruptive coloration, disguise, and mimicry.

DISRUPTIVE COLORATION

This is when an animal is striped or spotted, making it hard to see the animal's outline. Light colored patterns especially are often confused with spots of sunlight. This Hawksbill Sea Turtle has a sizzling shell that is distracting and confusing to its predators!

CONCEALING COLORATION

This is when an animal is the same color as its environment, making it difficult to find. By sitting motionlessly for a long period of time, the animal is relatively safe, but any movement may give it away. This Moon Jelly is translucent like the water, and this Reticulate Whipray can blend in with the sea floor!

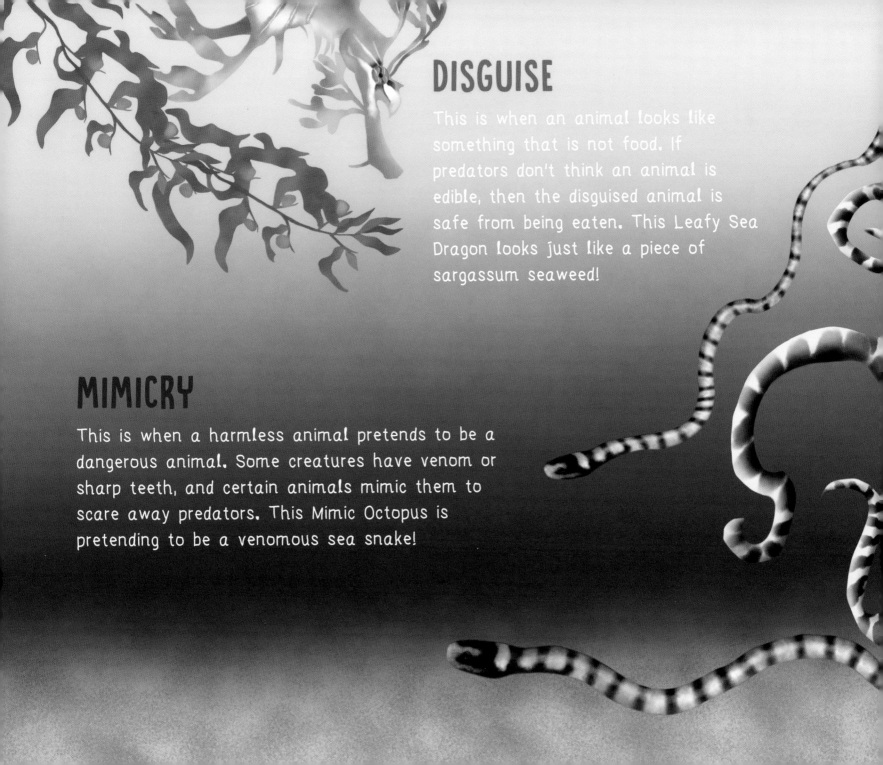

DISGUISE

This is when an animal looks like something that is not food. If predators don't think an animal is edible, then the disguised animal is safe from being eaten. This Leafy Sea Dragon looks just like a piece of sargassum seaweed!

MIMICRY

This is when a harmless animal pretends to be a dangerous animal. Some creatures have venom or sharp teeth, and certain animals mimic them to scare away predators. This Mimic Octopus is pretending to be a venomous sea snake!

DID YOU SEA US?

PYGMY SEAHORSE

RETICULATE WHIPRAY

MOON JELLY

URCHIN CRAB

LEAFY SEA DRAGON

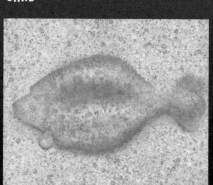

PEACOCK FLOUNDER

DID YOU SEA US?

HAWKSBILL SEA TURTLE

PIPEFISH

SARGASSUM SHRIMP, SARGASSUM CRAB, SARGASSUM FISH

MIMIC OCTOPUS

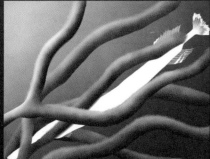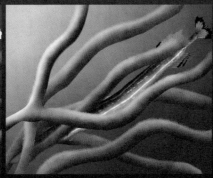

TRUMPETFISH

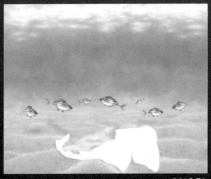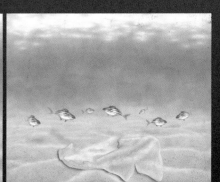

ANGEL SHARK